The GIRLS' DOODLE Book

Amazing Pictures to Complete and Create

Andrew Pinder

RP | KIDS
PHILADELPHIA

Illustrated by Andrew Pinder

Copyright © 2013 by Buster Books

All rights reserved under the Pan-American and International Copyright Conventions

First published in Great Britain in 2008 by Buster Books,
an imprint of Michael O'Mara Books Limited, 9 Lion Yard, Tremadoc Road, London SW4 7NQ.

First published in the United States by Running Press Book Publishers, 2008

Printed in China

Books published by Running Press are available at special discounts for bulk purchases in the United States by
corporations, institutions, and other organizations. For more information, please contact the
Special Markets Department at the Perseus Books Group, 2300 Chestnut Street, Suite 200, Philadelphia,
PA 19103, or call (800) 810-4145, ext. 5000, or e-mail special.markets@perseusbooks.com.

ISBN 978-0-7624-5290-3

16   15   14   13   12   11
Digit on the right indicates the number of this printing

Published by Running Press Book Publishers
An Imprint of Perseus Books, LLC.
A Subsidiary of Hachette Book Group, Inc.
2300 Chestnut Street
Philadelphia, PA 19103-4371

Visit us on the web!
www.runningpress.com/kids

Draw the best bouquet.

Give the fish a fabulous home.

Populate the penguin colony.

Create your perfect party cake.

Draw each dog a designer outfit.

Fill the hamsters' cage with fun.

fun

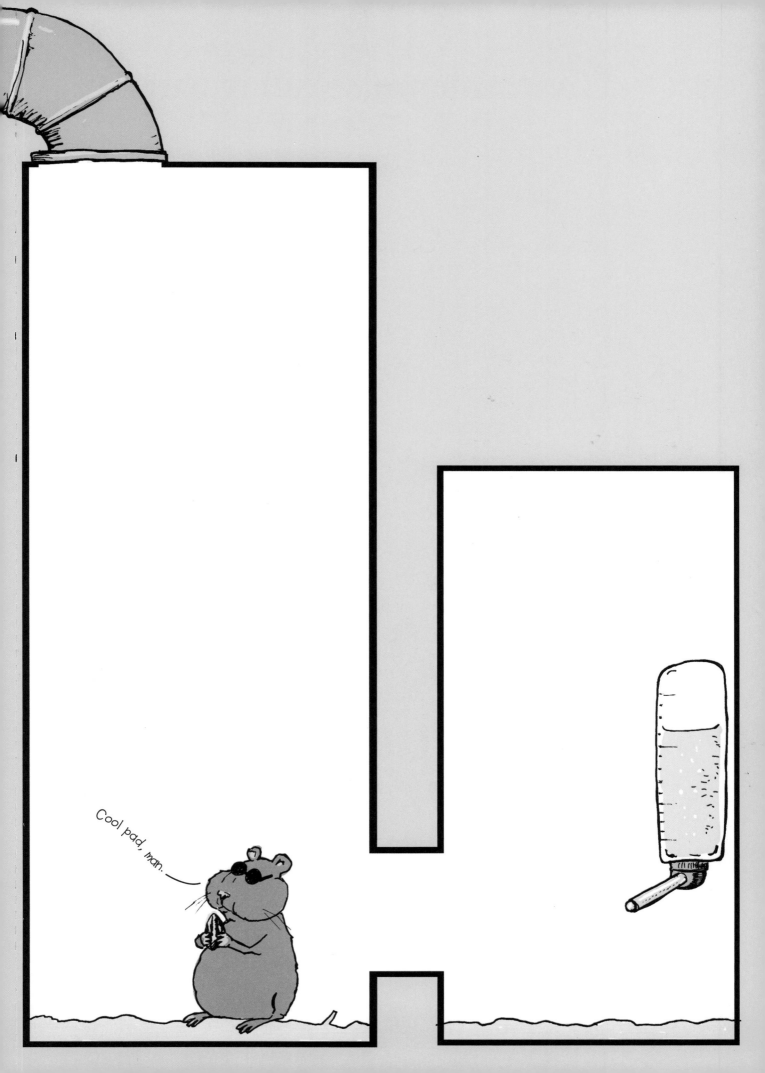

Give mademoiselle big hair.

Add a pal for the parrot.

Where are the fairies hiding?

Coming, ready or not.

What is Coco juggling?

Oh, no! What has Gran knitted now?

Fill the pond with lilies.

Decorate her hands with henna.

What do you see in the crystal ball?

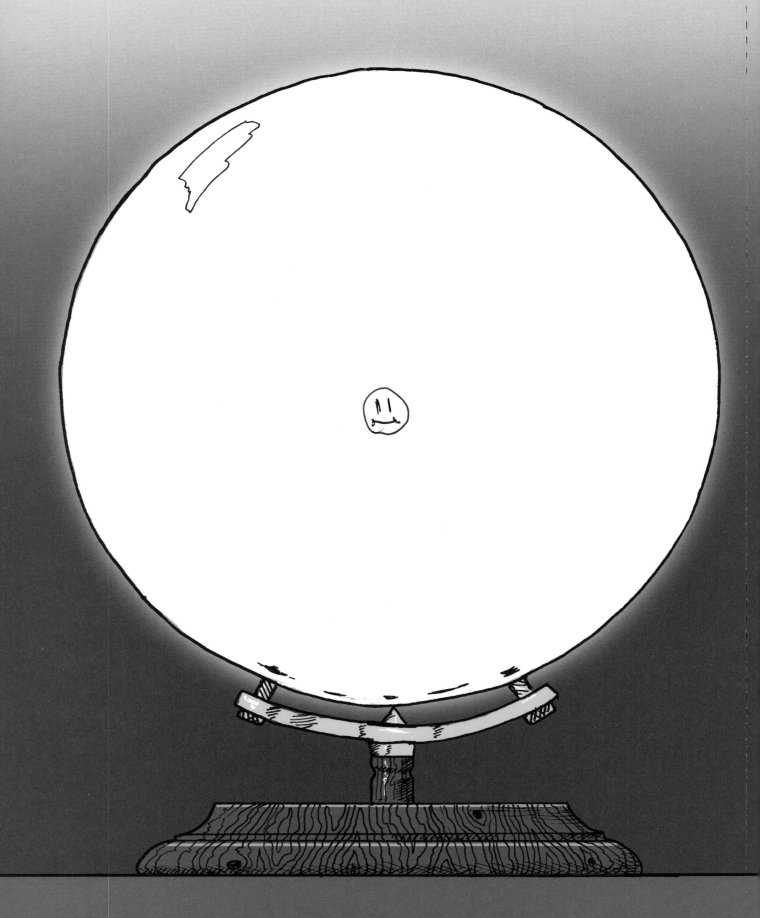

Shower the diva with flowers.

Imagine a mermaid's treasure.

It's mine, all mine.

Design the world's coolest phone.

What has she built on the beach?

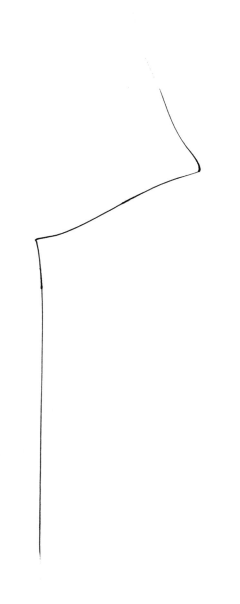

Who is in the burrow?

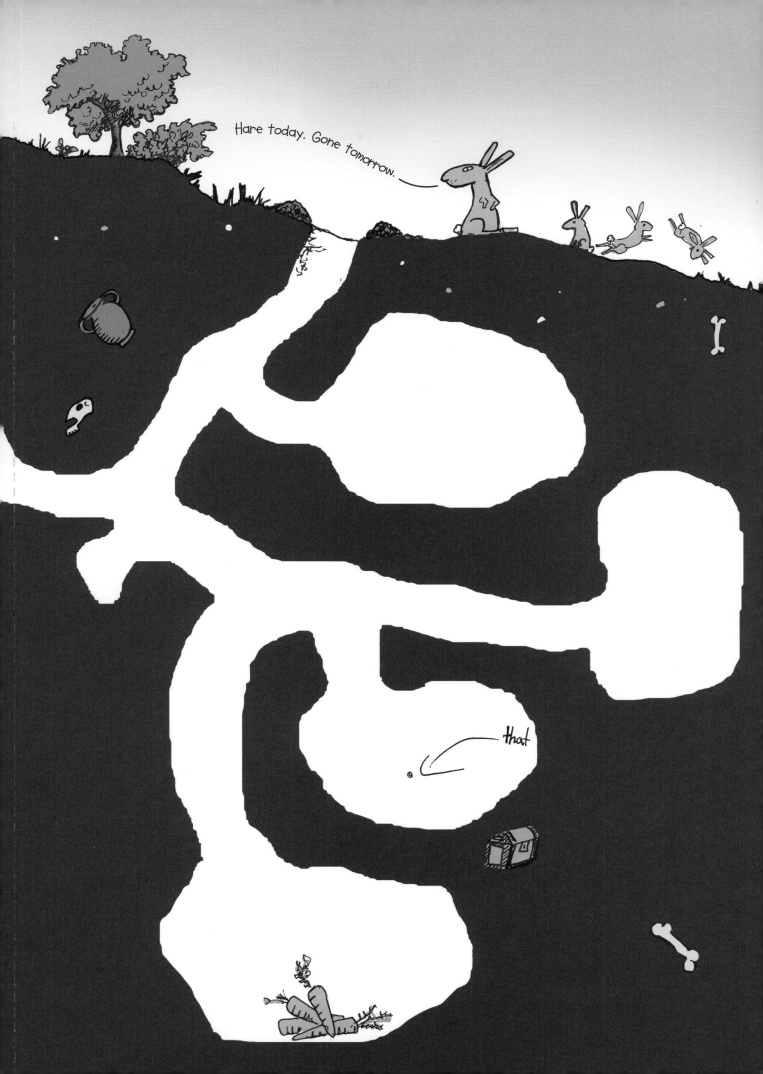

What are the dogs chasing?

Say cheese!

Draw the world's biggest and rarest butterfly.

What is she balancing on?

Design her super-costume . . . and one for the cat.

I'm cat-tastic. I have super meowers!

Design a CD cover and a T-shirt for her band.

Can you complete the carousel?

Faster, faster.

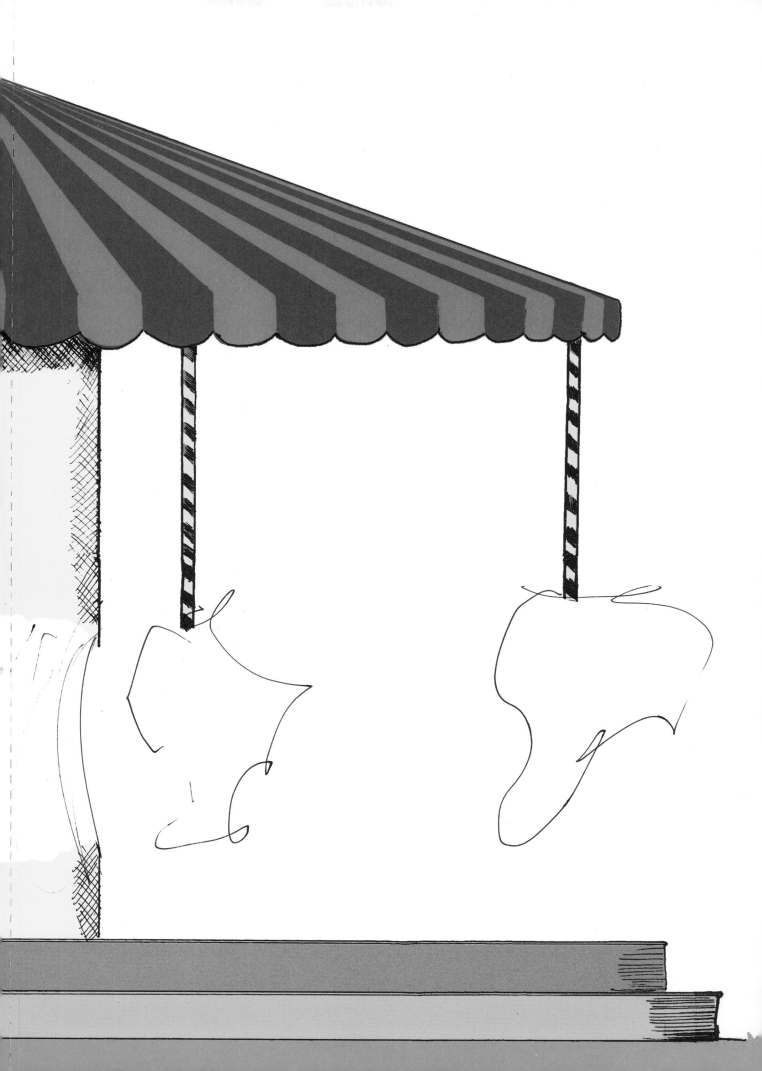

Draw Bo Peep's sheep.

Don't tell me you lost them again!

Draw a leaping dolphin.

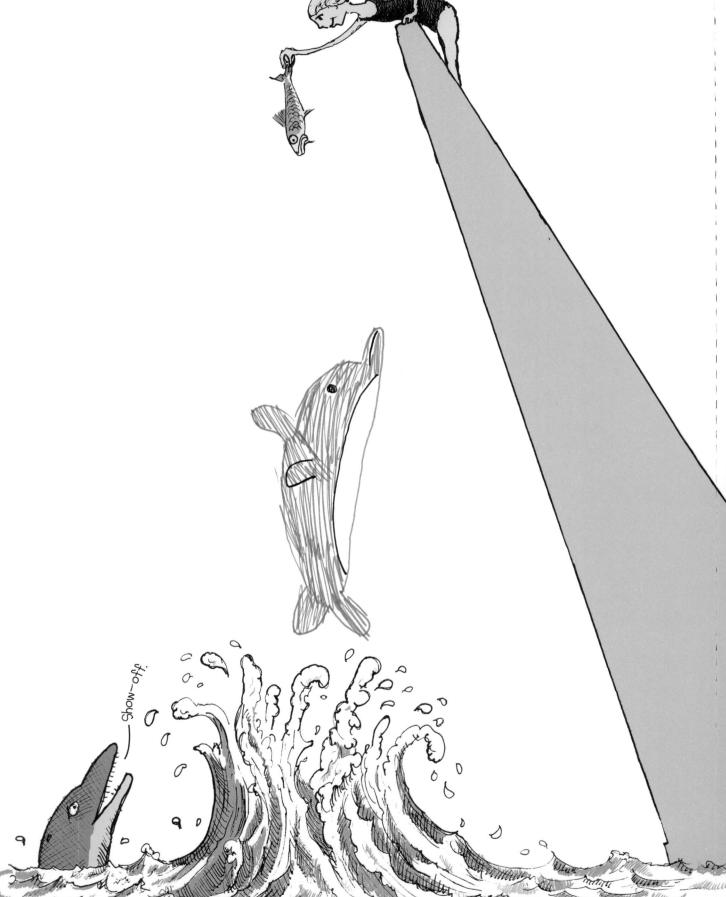

Show-off.

Beads and braids.

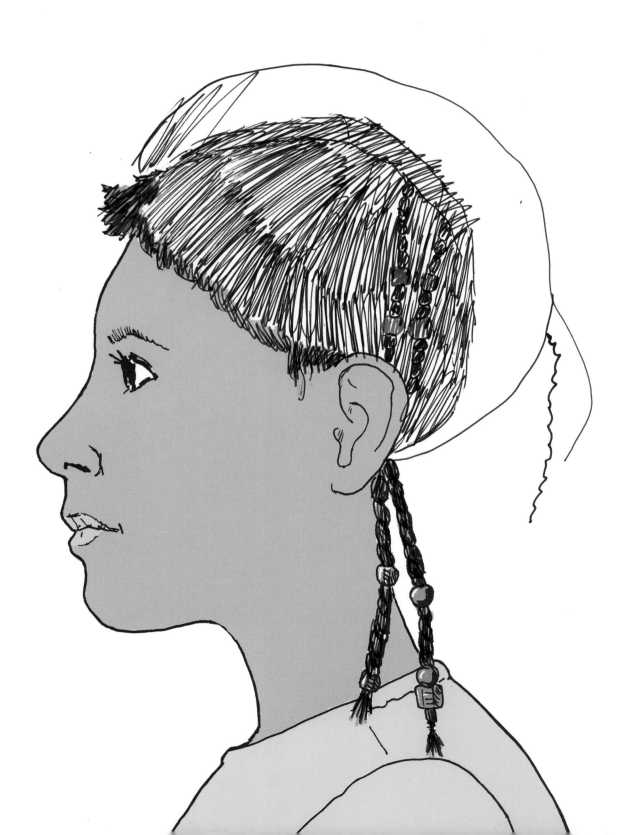

Abracadabra!

Dad, are you in there?

Design a fancy costume.

Are the bathrooms really upstairs?

How will you save the kitten?

Who is balancing on the beam?

Decorate the box with shells.

Help!

Paint their faces,
fans, and kimonos.

Put on a puppet show.

Who laid these eggs?

Finish building these igloos.

Picture a beach paradise.

Aloha!

Build a
tree house
fit for fairies.

Can you finish the maze?

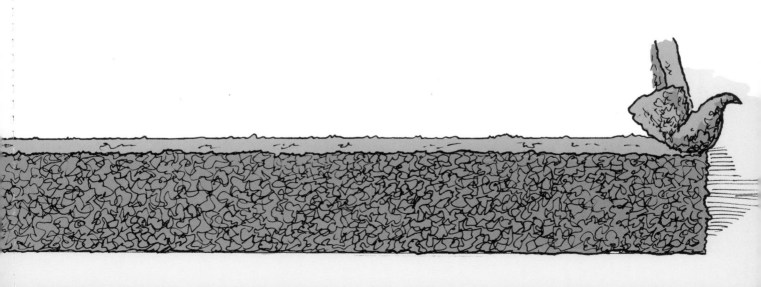

Decorate their teepees.

What would you take to a desert island?

Welcome to Tortoise Island.

Finish the slide.

The smaller the better.

Draw some
miniature masterpieces.

What can they see on the ghost train?

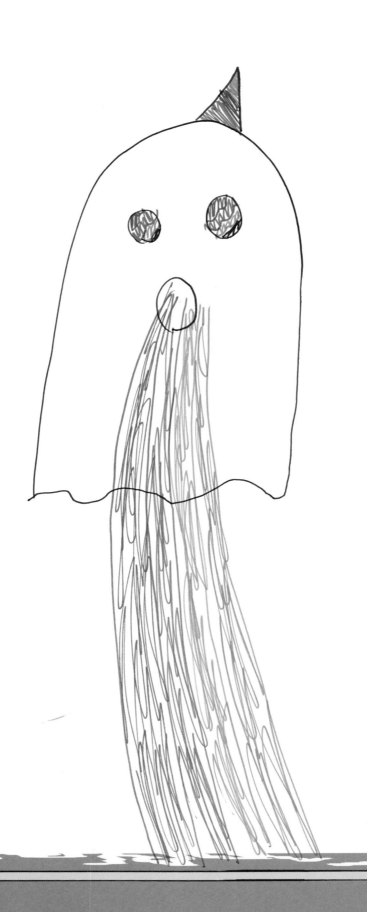

Decorate their saris . . .

but don't forget the elephant's coat.

When it is complete, make a wish.

Finish the daisy chain.

Design the
world's most
valuable tiara.

Make the sunflowers grow.

Complete this comic strip.

Put a tail on the bird of paradise.

What can they see in
this winter wonderland?

What is in your sandwich?

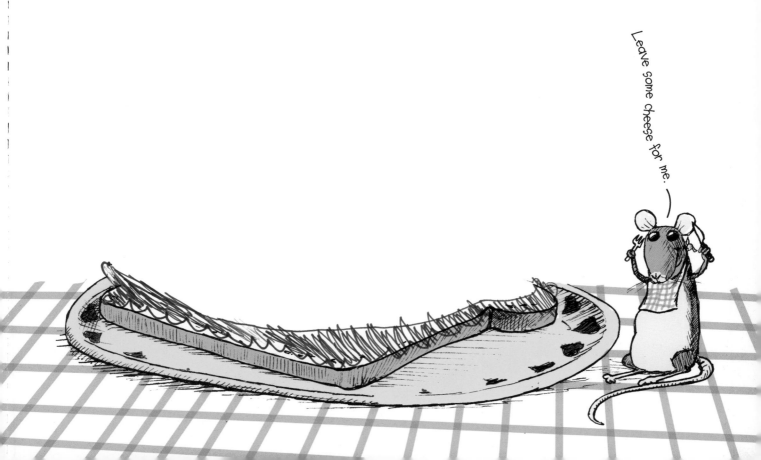

Leave some cheese for me.

Who is walking by the café window?

Such a beautiful bride!

What happened to her homework?

What is playing at the movies?

Who is driving the car?

Design the cheerleaders' outfits.

Finish the gingerbread house.

Draw the kittens in the shop.

How many butterflies are there?

Where is she landing?

Twirl her ribbon.

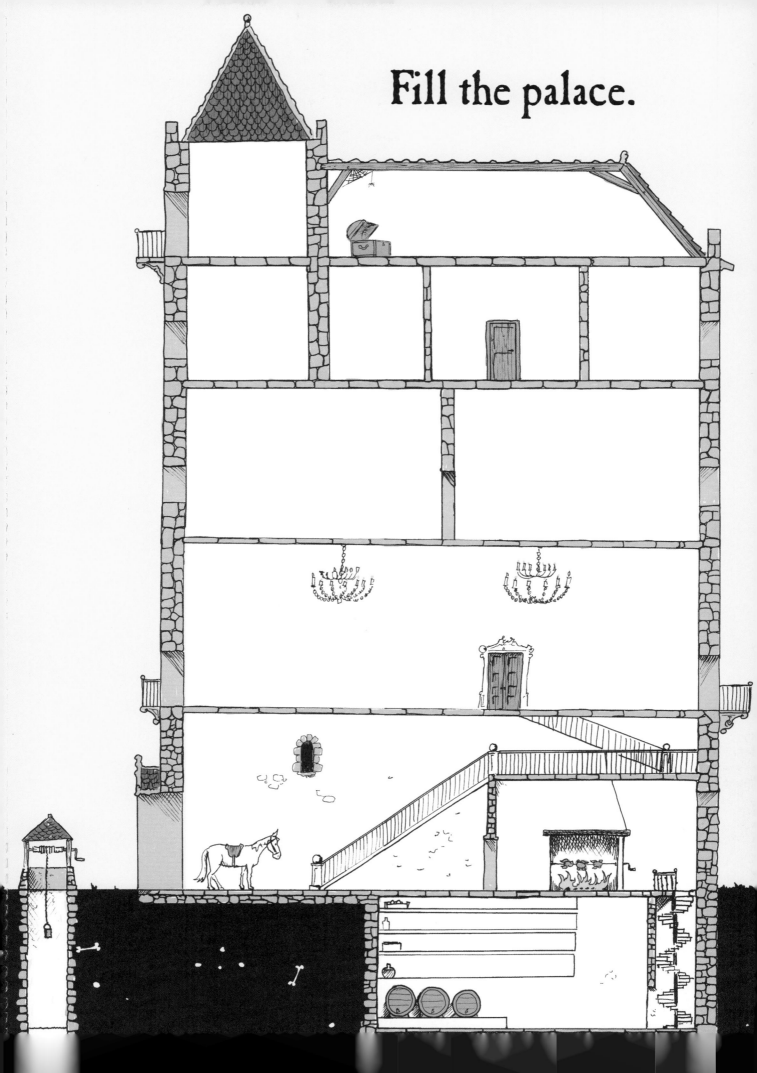

Fill the palace.

What is below the balloon?

Yummy!

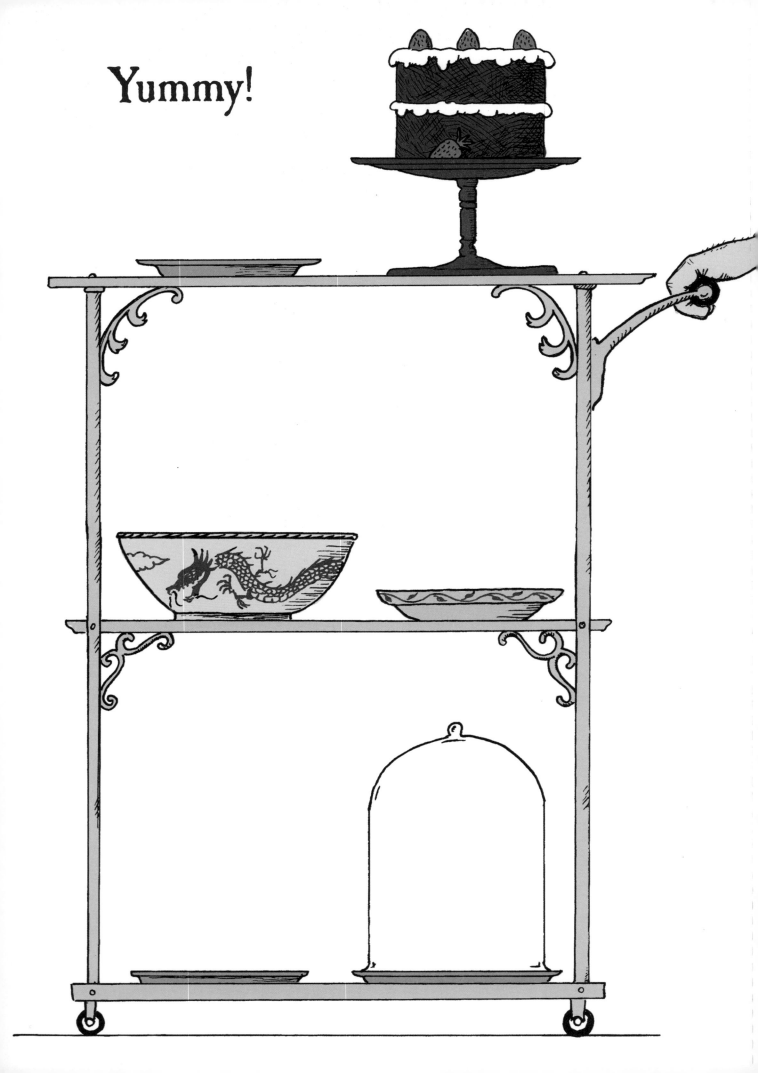

Who is sailing the boat?

Show a spectacular dive.

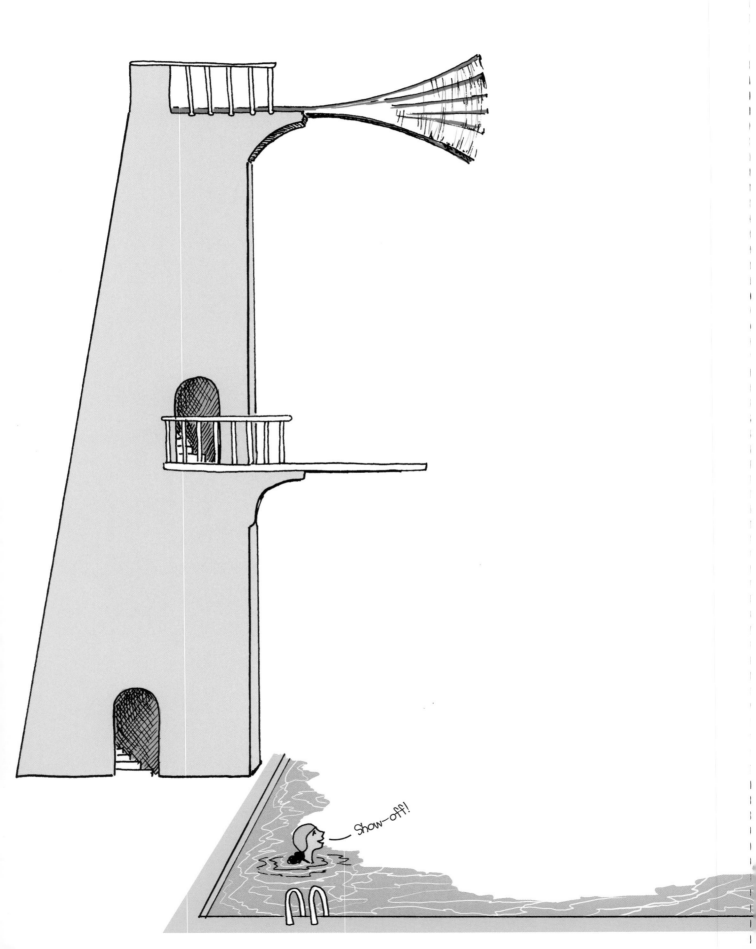

Build the world's biggest snowman.

Design a completely new pet.

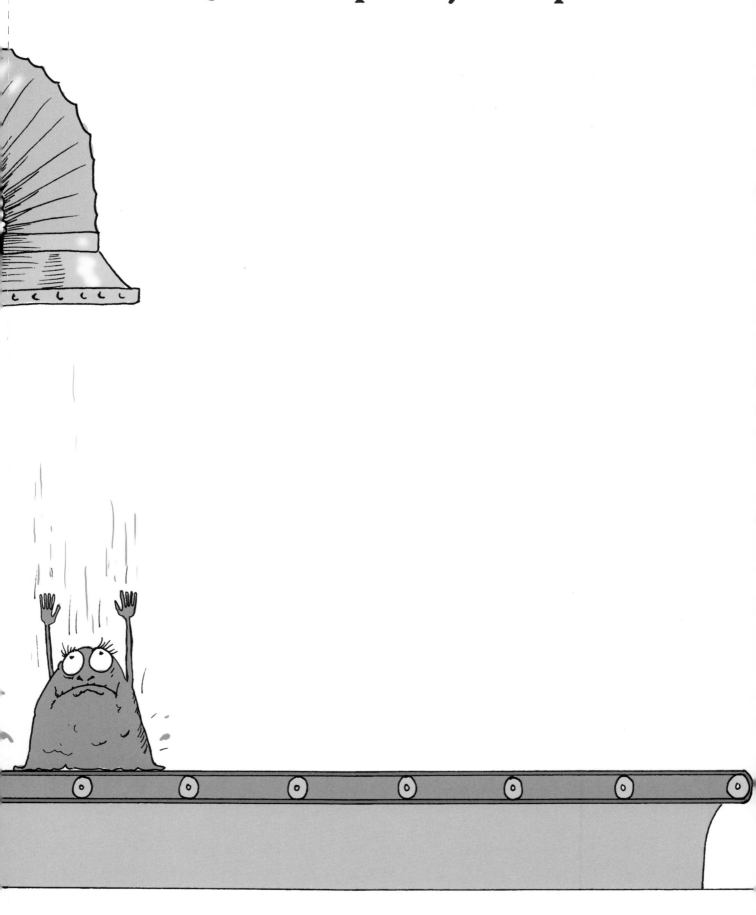

Who are they
following?

Who is sitting in the swingboats?

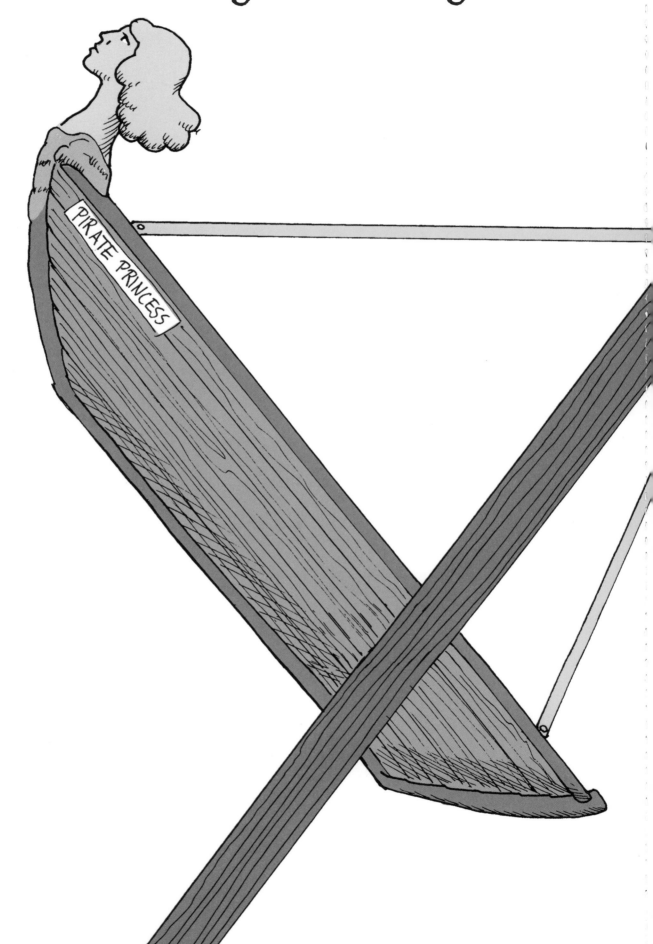

PIRATE PRINCESS

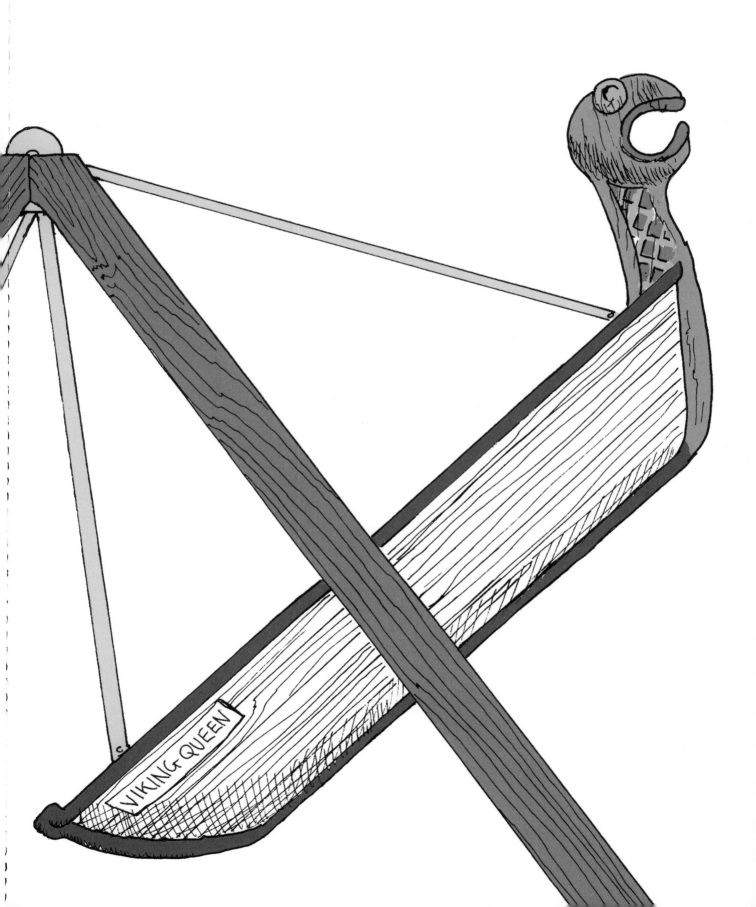

What has escaped from the zoo?

They went that way. Honest.

Who's kicking up the leaves?

Relax!

What is the princess sleeping on?

Who is crossing the rope bridge?

Fill the trees with woodland creatures.

Fill the shelves with toys.

Put Cleopatra on her throne.

How will she get down?

Windsurfer girls.

Fill the sweets jars . . .

and the chocolate boxes.

Complete the street.

Who is coming to town with the circus?

Decorate the beach hut.

What have the three little pigs built now?

What an enormous bunch of flowers!

What has washed up on the beach?

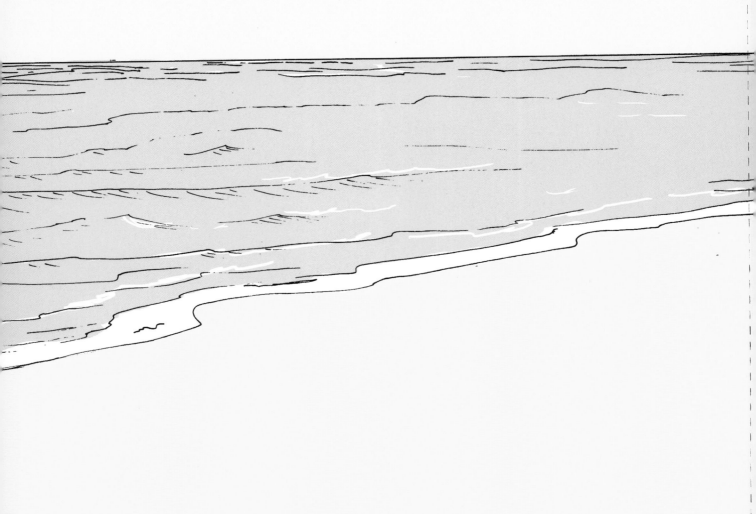

Help her paint the caravan.

Who is floating up, up, and away?

What has the baby built?

Design your own really cool chess set.

King

Queen

Bishop

Put the finishing touches on the cuckoo clock.

Nice frame, not sure about the picture.

What an amazing painting!

Which pooches are prize-winning pets?

BEST DOG

BIGGEST DOG

SMALLEST
DOG

BEST HAIRCUT

Do they eat dogs as well?

Ha, ha—they don't eat girls.

Oh no, man-eating plants. Run!

Who's traveling on the Egyptian barge?

Who is the fairest of them all?

Fill the pool with toys.

Mouse invasion!

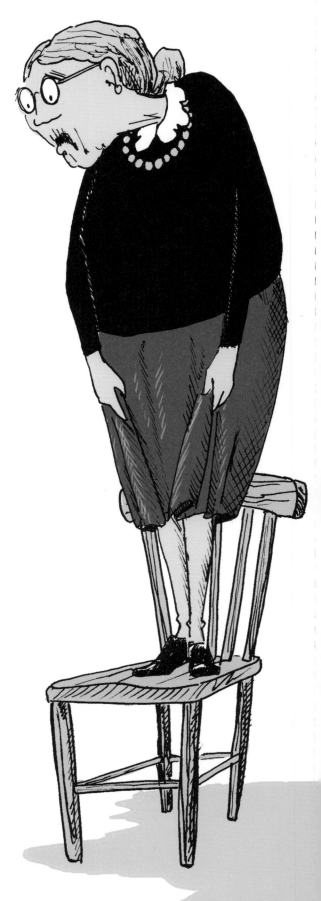

Who is making the baby cry?

Draw Spy-Girl's secret weapon.

Doodle everyone a tail.

Mine is the waggiest.

Mine is the fluffiest.

Mine is the bushiest.

Mine is all tail.

Mine is the most beautiful.

Mine is the thinnest.

Mine is the flattest.
Mine is the curliest.
Mine is the most useful.
Mine is the scariest.

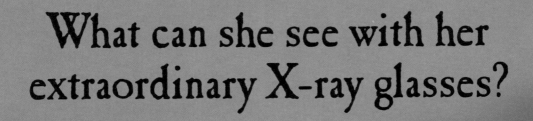

What can she see with her
extraordinary X-ray glasses?

The world's only dancing-tortoise troupe.

What will you wish for at the wishing well?

What is in the cart at the toy shop?